How to Resist Temptation

David R. Mains

David C. Cook Publishing Co.

ELGIN, ILLINOIS—WESTON, ONTARIO

HOW TO RESIST TEMPTATION
© 1980 David R. Mains
All rights reserved. Except for brief excerpts for review purposes,
no part of this book may be reproduced without written permission
from the publisher.

All Scripture quotations are from the Revised Standard Version
unless otherwise noted.

Published by David C. Cook Publishing Co., Elgin, IL 60120
Cover design by Joe Ragont
Printed in the United States of America
ISBN 0-89191-258-4
LC 80-51276

CONTENTS

The Chapel Talks Series by David Mains

Making Church More Enjoyable
How to Support Your Pastor
How to Resist Temptation
God, Help Us with the Kids
What's Wrong with Lukewarm?
Praying More Effectively
Getting to Know the Holy Spirit
When God Gets Angry with a Nation
A Closer Walk with God
Psalms That Touch Us Where We Live
Making Scripture Yours
I Needed That Encouragement

INTRODUCTION

Most people listen to the radio while they're doing something else. As a broadcaster I'm aware that a person hearing me is probably shaving, fixing breakfast, driving to work, or some similar activity. Being able to keep his or her attention in such a setting is a lot different than preaching to a captive audience.

Therefore, I was dubious as to whether the slow pace of radio with its need for frequent repetition and underscoring each key truth would transfer all that well into print.

To complicate matters further, every time a program is made I must assume many listeners didn't hear what was said the day before. But just the opposite is true when compiling the chapters of a book. They build on one another.

Well, the first series of Chapel talks is now completed. Through the help of others, my broadcast scripts have been made more readable than I thought possible. The greatest thanks for this project goes to my wife, Karen, who put aside her own writing to help me out. Two Chapel of the Air staff members, Ruby Christian and Sharon Morse, also did yeoman duty typing long hours after work and on weekends.

1

TEMPTATION VS. SIN

I can't remember a day when I haven't been consciously tempted in one way or another. Temptation will be part of this day as well, and I'm afraid tomorrow won't be any different. That's because being tempted is a normal part of being alive. One could wish it were otherwise, but wishing won't do any good.

I don't mean to imply that I'm bombarded relentlessly from dawn till dusk. If that were the case, I think I'd examine myself to discover what I'm doing wrong. Even though Satan is rightly called "the tempter," I can still set myself up for disaster by unwise choices of what I look at, listen to, smell, touch, or even think. Therefore, my policy has been that the less I contribute to such problems the better. I often pray as Jesus taught: "Father, please help me not to be led into temptation." Nevertheless, it still comes my way often enough.

Scripture reports that temptation was also a part of Christ's experience. The Book of Hebrews says that in every respect he was "tempted as we are, yet without sin" (Heb. 4:15). Since Christ was sinless, there has to be a difference between being tempted and committing sin.

Temptation is usually thought of as the initial enticement, while sin is an actual yielding to the evil. In a sense, because temptation can be overcome and thus bring positive results in a life, it could possibly be classified as a neutral experience—depending on how one responds to it. (Something inside me, however, reacts against this approach and warns that one is wise to treat temptation carefully and avoid it whenever possible).

Precisely when temptation ends and sin begins is not always easy to determine. Nevertheless, the two are not to be confused with each other. An illustration may clarify things.

When I was a boy my favorite treat was mom's chocolate-chip cookies. On occasion she would bake at the same time she prepared dinner. Playing nearby, I could smell them while they were still in the oven. "Now, David, you're not to touch the cookies until after supper," she would say, putting them on the counter to cool. I had no problem with that as long as mom didn't leave the room.

If she did (especially if she went outside or over to dad's office across the drive), sometimes strange influences seemed to take over my young mind. While I continued playing, my nostrils would pick up the heavenly aroma. Before long, my normally innocent brain was searching desperately for a way to get some of those cookies off the baking sheets without leaving any evidence.

Now that difficulty in itself should have stopped me, because it's not an easy trick to pull off unless—Maybe I could blame it on my brother or sister! Or the dog! I could pretend she had knocked a whole tin off the counter. No, I would have to do better than that. And before you know it, a plan was in careful operation, the evidence rearranged. Good; and now for that first scrumptious bite!

"David Randall, put that cookie down!" Uhhh—how did mother always time her return so perfectly?

Was I sinning? I didn't actually take a bite! The answer is still yes. Why? Because I had disobeyed my mother.

When had the sin begun? I'm not really sure. Possibly it was while I thought too long about how I could do what I knew I wasn't supposed to, instead of concentrating on obeying my mother. But whenever the line was crossed, I do know it wasn't as I thought, *M-m-m-m, one of those cookies would sure taste good right now.* That thought was temptation, it wasn't sin.

It would have been foolish at that point to have said, "O God, forgive me for such a wicked idea," because the thought in itself was merely a temptation.

Talking about cookies may sound elementary, but the same kind of situation occurs in the mind of a man who comes for counseling regarding impure thoughts. "Reverend Mains, I need help. Even when I'm on my knees praying, sometimes the most immoral pictures enter my head!"

The enemy still does everything he can to keep people from praying, doesn't he? It could well be that such a person needs to be more scrupulous in eliminating anti-Christian sexual stimulation. There's an awful lot of this around in newspapers, magazines, and television programs, even those considered kosher by most people.

Nevertheless, having the thought in itself is not a defeat. The question is: What do you do with it? Do you encourage it? Do you roll it back and forth in your mind like the little boy who drools over a forbidden cookie? Or do you think almost immediately, *This is not something for me to entertain; I turn my back on it and say, "No, Satan, begone with your tainted wares!" God, help me now as I seek to honor you.*

That's the proper course. How foolish to give up before the battle has even begun! We must understand that temptation is nothing more than the enemy getting our attention through subtlety of one kind or another. We can hardly prevent him from doing this. But we can learn to respond, "Get out of here. I don't have time for liars."

"Wait a minute, David," you say. "It's not as though he whispers or talks quietly. When I close my eyes he seems to plant vivid pictures in my head." Then open your eyes and pictures will vanish!

Also, be aware that many temptations are related to visual stimulation. Let's conduct an experiment. I'm going to mention a word, and I want you to think of what the word means without visualizing what it represents.

The word is *hippopotamus*. Did you think of the word without picturing the object? Probably not. That's because many words automatically bring to mind pictures of what they symbolize.

For example, I don't doubt but what Jesus, hungry after forty days of fasting, saw for a moment the warm, yeasty, fragrant bread Satan suggested he should create from stones in front of him. But immediately the thought, with its powerful visual reminder, was set aside by the great answer, "It is written, Man shall not live by bread alone, but by every word that proceeds from the mouth of God" (Matt. 4:4).

What I'm saying is, treat temptation, not as something about which you feel guilty, but rather as a clear signal to begin immediate God-honoring action. That's because once temptation is recognized, and quickly put aside, the greater your chances of victory.

Backing up another step, what I'm hoping to get across is that *healthy Christians understand the difference between temptation and sin.*

For example, the moment you recognize feelings of jealousy rising, don't ask for forgiveness. At that point you haven't yet done anything wrong. Identify the source of the suggestion and say, "No, thank you, Satan, I don't care for any of that. I've tried it before, and though it seems to taste good at first, it always upsets my stomach later. Offer it to somebody else if you must, but you'll not dish it up here."

Revenge. Getting even. "It sure seems appropriate after what she did to you, doesn't it?" (*Oh,* you think, *I know that voice.*)

Now respond. "Sorry. My Lord says, 'Beloved, never avenge yourselves, but leave it to the wrath of God; for it is written, "Vengence is mine, I will repay, says the Lord" (Rom. 12:19).

No. "If your enemy is hungry, feed him; if he is thirsty,

give him drink: for by doing so you will heap burning coals upon his head" (Rom. 12:20).

So I say, "Thank you, Mr. Devil, for the reminder that something should be done. But today I'm taking God's advice."

There are even times when mid-course corrections can be made in conversations before the temptation is allowed to become sin. In talking with people, thoughts often come out of our mouths the same moment they come to our minds. You stretch the truth, and recognize it even as you speak the words. Correct it instantly. Don't allow the temptation to become sin by letting the exaggeration remain unchallenged.

"Your average is 162, huh? Well, my bowling must be about that too—oops, that's too high. Better make it what it was last season—138. But I still enjoy the game!" Then don't mope because you fell. Instead, rejoice because you were victorious! You recognized temptation and overcame it.

Am I making myself clear? Temptation is a normal part of life. If it overwhelms you, there's probably something you're doing to encourage it. But if it's there just occasionally throughout the day, don't feel guilty. Look at it as a sign of the enemy's real presence; then refuse to toy with it.

Think of temptation as something to step around, like confronting a poisonous snake that coils and says, "Did God s-s-say this-s was-s not good for you? Let me open your eyes-s."

My prayer is that you will remember these simple thoughts about temptation the next time you hear the enemy's hiss.

2

THE DEVIL'S DESIRE

Here's a short poem by the American humorist, Ogden Nash, entitled "The Panther."

The panther is like the leopard,
 but he isn't peppered.
When you see a panther crouch,
 prepare to say "ouch!"
Better still, when called by a panther,
 don't anther.

This same logic is given, only in a more profound setting, by the Apostle Peter in his first New Testament epistle. He writes about a lion, but the warning is the same. Beware of beasts with bad reputations.

See if this is not what he is saying. Here is 1 Peter 5:8, 9a from the Living Bible: "Be careful—watch out for attacks from Satan, your great enemy. He prowls around like a hungry, roaring lion, looking for some victim to tear apart. Stand firm when he attacks. Trust the Lord."

Now I know that temptation is a traveling companion of every person. It has no regard for age, sex, race, income, education, nationality, or religion. The enemy slights no one with his allurements, and certainly this generation hasn't been overlooked. Yet it is amazing to me that since life and temptation run a parallel course, so few, including Christians, have formulated definite plans as to how they will face it. Maybe I should make the discussion more personal. What defense do *you* presently employ when the hungry lion growls?

In the next three chapters I will offer some simple but effective truths that come directly from 1 Peter 5:8, 9a. Once learned, they can be drawn upon again and again at short notice.

Let me remind you once again of the difference between being tempted and sinning. Temptation is the trumpets sounding. It is the battle flags being hoisted and the troops quickly being aligned. One can then win or lose, and the outcome is usually determined quickly. Temptation can certainly result in sin, but victory is just as real an option. Therefore temptation and sin are not necessarily the same.

In a sentence, my basic thought for this chapter is: *To be alert during temptation, one must know the enemy.* Listen again to Peter's words: "Be careful—watch out for attacks from Satan, your great enemy. He prowls around like a hungry, roaring lion looking for some victim to tear apart." Satan's desire is to destroy.

Of course, in real life, the seducer doesn't introduce

himself with, "Hello there, my desire is to destroy you!" More generally he appears as a reasonable and understanding friend, a sympathizer. I know that he will provide me with all kinds of plausible excuses to take whatever cheap prize he happens to be pandering. He dangles before my mind such thoughts as:

"David, God doesn't expect you to be perfect. He knows you love him. This is such a small thing."

"David, think how hard you have been going, the pressure you are under, how much you serve the Lord! Who doesn't deserve a break now and then?"

"David, you know a church leader who is plagued with this problem and everybody excuses him."

"David, think how they treated you."

"David, most people wouldn't even consider this a sin."

"David, God made you with certain drives, it's just natural."

Now the deceiver never mentions how transitory is the pleasure he offers. Nothing of the resultant guilt is communicated, or what his finished products look like. Scriptures aren't brought up. Rather, one after another, reasonable excuses are suggested for me to do what I normally would feel I should not do. Yet all the time, in spite of the sweet talk, Satan's real desire is to destroy me.

You know what I have discovered? The instant I yield and sample his bait, everything immediately changes. In a moment he is at my throat.

"Ah ha, look at you now, David. You knew that was wrong before you did it, didn't you! Look at you now, the one who is supposed to be a minister, tells others how to overcome! Just a little while back didn't you promise God you would never do this again if he would forgive you? Did it anyway, didn't you! Hey, David, why don't you just give up?"

Then, of course, it all fits so clearly into place. His desire all along was to destroy. He never was my friend. This dirty deceiver had been plotting my ruin, purposing to bring about my downfall.

The sooner I ingrain in my mind that Satan's desire is to destroy, the better off I am. To be alert during temptation, one must know the enemy. It is a requirement. We have no choice but to be watchful. We must recognize the intent of the evil one. We must understand that Satan wants to destroy us.

Let us think about you. Now I know you are tempted—and there is nothing wrong with that. But the question is: How are you handling the temptation? Do you have a strategy to keep you on your guard? Have you formed any kind of plans to stay out of the lion's jaws? Well, let's personalize what I have been sharing.

What temptation most repeatedly troubles you? That shouldn't take too long to answer, whether it is greed, worry, lust, uncontrolled anger, gluttony, laziness, or arrogance.

When you have pinpointed your major weakness, and are aware of where the enemy likes to attack, the next question is: *When will this temptation most likely occur next?*

"How am I supposed to know that?" you ask.

Well, think about it for a minute. You may not be able to pinpoint the exact day and time, but you can predict that the next occasion you are with so-and-so, or when the name of the person you don't like comes up in conversation, you will be tempted. Maybe it is at mealtime, the day of the month that a specific magazine is issued, when you are in a certain part of town, or when you are tired and all alone. Attempt to get a better handle on when you feel the temptation will likely next occur.

With this as a background, begin the process of being on the alert so temptation will not catch you by surprise. In order for you to be ready when the enemy makes himself known, remind yourself all through the day, *Satan's desire is to destroy me through his temptation.* When you rise, whisper, "Satan will want to destroy me today." When you pray before a meal, breathe, "Father, help me to remember through your Spirit the enemy's true intent." Write the warning on a card placed where you will see it often if that helps. Satan's desire is to destroy. Ask a friend to repeat the truth often. In fact, say it out loud right now. "Satan's desire is to destroy."

Before you go to bed at night, thank God for revealing this certainty to you about the father of lies—that his desire is to destroy you. In time, this basic spiritual fact will begin to be written on your mind. The world may laugh, but you know that for too long the devil has defeated you in times past.

Satan means no good by you. He has one purpose and that is to shame you. The sooner this is fixed in your mind, the better off you are going to be.

Having prepared yourself in this manner, when you sense the deceiver is near you certainly must not fail to repeat what you have been saying—*Satan's desire is to destroy.* Because, believe it or not, he is clever enough to still entice you to grab at the charms he dangles.

Sure, you enjoy buying things even though you can't afford them. Stretching the truth is gratifying if it makes you look better. Cutting others with your tongue, taking advantage of someone, playing with lust in your mind. But you dare not. Why? You give me the answer. That's right, Satan's desire is to destroy.

Your immediate response to temptation should be, "I can't. It is too perilous. I have felt his fangs sink into me before. I've been too often a plaything in his paws. I won't give in. I am not interested."

I don't want to give you the impression that an alert attitude is in itself enough to overcome temptation. It is only a beginning. In the next chapters we will look at other parts of a plan to overcome the devil's desire.

3

A GREAT OPPORTUNITY

Is temptation positive or negative?

If defeat is the result of such confrontations in your life, you will probably answer the latter. But did you know that many people who enjoy a healthy walk with Christ actually see these occasions as opportunities to prove God's promises? Though they don't invite such face-offs, they certainly aren't cowed by them either. Rather, in the pattern established by Christ in the wilderness, they beat Satan at his own game.

You will remember that Peter advised his readers, "Be careful—watch out for attacks from Satan, your great enemy. He prowls around like a hungry, roaring lion, looking for some victim to tear apart. Stand firm when he attacks. Trust the Lord" (1 Pet. 5:8, 9a, The Living Bible).

After warning you that during temptation you should be aware that Satan desires to destroy you, Peter next advises: "Stand firm when he attacks."

This statement indicates that you don't have to lose because victory is an available option. In other words, you are not obliged to acquiesce to evil. Rather, if you choose, you *can* overcome. In fact, if every temptation were to be removed from your life, it's difficult to say how much real growth would occur in you as a follower of Christ.

The apostle's emphasis here is that *to be alert during temptation, one must recognize an opportunity.* That opportunity, of course, is to overcome. Otherwise, why would the author write, "Stand firm when he attacks"?

I fear this truth is not as deeply imbedded in Christian minds as it should be. Once it begins to take root, however, temptation is no longer viewed as something to be bitterly endured, but rather as a great challenge to be accepted. After all, God's people are promised that he will never allow them to be tempted above what they are able to stand. What has happened, then, to this basic indicator of growth among believers? And where did the spirit of confidence go?

When I was a youngster, there was no tv. I was a part of the last generation to watch radio! That was all you could do. In Quincy, Illinois, where I lived as a boy, I used to stop whatever I was doing a little before 3:30 P.M. At that time the "Lone Ranger" came on the air. At 3:45 P.M. a foghorn sounded; then the announcer would say, "Presenting Captain Midnight and the Secret Squadron!" At least that is how my memory reconstructs it. Four o'clock began with a cymbal crash and "Terry and the Pirates!"

Finally it was 4:15. Time for my favorite, the greatest

cowboy who ever lived, Tom Mix. "Take a tip from Tom, tell your mom, hot Ralston can't be beat." Remember the theme song? It is a shame youngsters today have never heard of him! Why Tom Mix could figure out in two weeks mysteries it would have taken the Lone Ranger several months to solve—even with Tonto's help!

I was the champion neighborhood listener on North Twenty-seventh Street. I had never missed a Tom Mix show for over two years! Then one day my little German grandmother came to stay with us. She was very special, and I have nothing but the fondest memories of her. But grandmother had certain ideas. To her, there was something sacred about family meals. Everyone was to be present, and there were to be no foreign elements allowed, such as books, comics, newspapers, toys—or even radio programs.

One day about 3:45 P.M. I heard sounds in the kitchen that told me grandmother was getting an early supper ready. Realizing that a conflict with my favorite program was in the making, I took a break during the Captain Midnight Ovaltine commercial, went into the kitchen, and asked in my most polite voice, "Little German grandmother, would you mind if I remained a loyal listener to the Tom Mix show during supper tonight? You see, I have a string of over two years of faithful hearing, and . . ."

Unfortunately, she minded. Next, plan two went into effect. I threw one whale of a temper tantrum. That technique also came up short! As embarrassing as it is for me to admit, my hero, Tom Mix, ended up badly beaten by my tiny German grandmother!

Now suppose I had never overcome my fixation for this program. You have come to counsel personally with me about a spiritual problem, traveling some distance to get to my office. After three quarters of an hour, I look at my watch and say, "Oh, my, I'm sorry but I'm going to have to leave in a couple of minutes in order to beat the traffic. You see, I need to be home at 4:10, and I dare not be late. Could we meet again tomorrow? But just a little earlier so I can leave at this same time. I have a daily radio program I don't want to miss."

"Well," you say, "I guess I could stay over one night." Then you ask, "What is the program?"

"It's just a little something special I've been listening to for many years," I respond, grabbing my coat and briefcase.

But you persist, becoming more intrigued as I continue to be evasive.

Finally I give in. "Well, you see, some years ago, even as a kid, I was a faithful listener at 4:15. Have you ever heard of Tom Mix? He's very good. Listen, I really must leave or I'll be late." And I'm on my way running to the car to get home on time to listen to you-know-what.

Well, you begin to think. *Isn't that something, every day Reverend Mains races home to hear Tom Mix's radio show! Why, if my memory serves me correctly, that old program was made for kids. I would think he would have outgrown it by now. In fact, what am I doing asking him for help?*

As you leave the office, you politely inform Lisa, the receptionist, "When Reverend Mains comes in tomorrow, please tell him I've changed my mind about seeing him. I think I'll just head for home!" And you go your way muttering in amazement, "Tom Mix!"

If all this sounds silly, you will understand how a minister sometimes feels. Often when we have counseled a person over an extended period of time, the thought arises that this current problem appears to be the same one this person talked about two years ago, and five years ago, and seven years ago. Different circumstances, perhaps, but it was the identical core, sin. In fact, if previous pastors could be contacted regarding the difficulties faced by this individual, is it not likely they would say that this exact flaw has been a lifetime disability?

It is as though some people don't realize that temptation can be overcome. They think when Satan pitches old number three, the only option they have is to swing weakly and miss! Why the enemy actually has church people convinced they are victims, that it is impossible to change. They will just have to reconcile themselves to stumbling and fumbling and bumbling around for as long as they live, believing that:

- A loose tongue can't be tamed by Christ.
- Certain worrying minds will never be able to find Jesus' peace.
- Long-standing bad habits must forever enslave.
- All Christians can't be expected to grow into maturity. Some must always remain religious juveniles.
- Stunted Christian growth is normal.
- None of us are ever really emotionally whole.

Nonsense! Every time you are tempted, you had better believe you have *every* opportunity to overcome. To be alert during temptation you must recognize an opportunity. You can grow up!

Others have. Joyce has gotten the victory over holding grudges.

Remember Ralph's hot temper? No more!

What has happened to Bill and Nancy? They used to spend money like it was going out of style. Now they really seem to have their shopping under control.

And what about you? What about the dawn of a new day in your life, my friend?

It will never occur if you don't change your attitude regarding temptation. Sure, there is a certain pleasure to sin. That is the reason people yield to temptation. Nobody sins out of obligation. They know their action affords satisfaction and gratification, of some kind or another.

But listen! There is a greater joy (immediate as well as far-ranging) from overcoming temptation than from yielding to it. Your opportunity is to overcome. Say it out loud: "When tempted, my opportunity is to overcome."

"But you don't know how hard . . .," you protest.

Yes I do. Save your comment and we will talk about it next chapter. For now, realize that what you have just read is God's truth stated in Scripture by the Apostle Peter. Don't destroy it! Slowly, but surely, let it start to permeate your mind.

4

SPECIAL HELP FROM A FRIEND

What temptations have you learned to overcome in the last half year?

I know that is a hard question to answer quickly, but suppose I gave you a minute or so? Do you think you would be able to name a sin that once characterized you, but in the last six months you have overcome?

My feeling is that most people would be forced to admit that some time in the past they put aside the idea of involving themselves in battle against difficult sins. Now they pretend that they are learning to grow spiritually. But when forced to think about it, they admit that they no longer have a serious intention of mastering such flaws.

Possibly during this reading God has been pleased to use these concepts to confront you on this matter. If that is true, it is because my thoughts come from words penned years ago by the Apostle Peter. Remember them: "Be careful—watch out for attacks from Satan, your great enemy. He prowls around like a hungry, roaring lion, looking for some victim to tear apart. Stand firm when he attacks. Trust the Lord."

Having talked about the enemy and yourself, we dare not overlook the fact that the great Friend of Christians is also present. "Trust the Lord," is how Peter puts it. So, *To be alert during temptation, one must trust a friend.* No believer needs to slog it out alone. In fact, to do so invites disaster. The enemy's advantage is too decided due to his experience, cunning, and power. But by introducing God into the battle, the growl of the beast on the prowl seems far less frightening.

When Peter says, "Trust the Lord," he is not saying we should always expect God to hear us screaming for help at the top of our lungs because the evil cat has pounced upon us and is chomping on a leg. In other words, the Lord does not want us to treat him as an impersonal can of spiritual mace that is always available to squirt at an attacker.

Possibly, that attitude is all right for brand new believers. But I am sure God wants to prepare his older children to be strong in battle so they won't enter into conflicts inexperienced and confused. Rather, they will be trained to know exactly how to respond, what maneuvers to follow—all the while demonstrating surprising confidence. Trusting the Lord, then, does not normally imply last minute frantic cries of panic, but a life patterned after a growing reliance on, or faith in, the Son of God—before, during, and after temptation. Let's give more attention to those words.

Victory over a sin that clings tenaciously usually isn't won without a battle royal. A successful outcome usually takes place in the first few seconds the temptation occurs. During that instant a person decides which voice he will allow to dominate, his friend's or his enemy's. Will she repeat the story even though she knows gossip is destructive? Or will she silence her lips? Said another way, will she be influenced by Satan's promptings about how good it will feel to tell one on so-and-so, or will she heed Christ's words—"Why do you see the speck that is in your sister's eye, but not notice the log that is in your own eye?"(See Matthew 7:3.)

Will he respond to the devious line for which so many have fallen in this twentieth century—to lust is to be a normal, healthy human being? Or will he side with Christ who said, "Everyone who looks at a woman lustfully has already committed adultery with her in his heart" (Matt. 5:28).

Peter's admonition is to trust the Lord.

Yet in a day characterized by subtle influences on our thoughts through the bombardment of the media, it is often far easier to pick up the pretender's lies than to remember the wise words of the Son of God. In order to not be captured in the stream of the damned, one needs to spend time with the true Friend of humans. His voice still speaks clearly enough to those who meditate on the Scriptures. In fact, if believers would invest one-half the time in the Bible that they do in tv, magazines, and newspapers, their lives would be radically transformed.

Certainly you realize that thirty minutes spent in a given newspaper each day will slowly influence you to think the way the editors do. Read every issue of a chosen magazine and over a time you will adopt much of the thinking of its staff. Spend hours weekly with tv and you will be conditioned by what you see. The change may be almost unnoticeable to you, but it will be taking place nevertheless. If believers today put greater emphasis on material things, are more permissive sexually, and are far less enamored with the church and its leaders, I am not surprised. It is a reflection of what they have been consuming.

Listen carefully, the "Tonight Show" may be relaxing to watch, but I am convinced it is not the best way to finish the day for someone who wants to walk close to God. The morning newspaper can be informative, but it does little to prepare a person spiritually for the hours ahead. Sunday morning church attendance usually has profitable input, but too often its value is offset by how one spends the rest of the day. I am saying that not enough Christians think of how they can hear Christ's voice over the din of the world. Little wonder so few are conscious of recent victories. In the midst of their full days they no longer have time to allow God's Spirit to school them in His thoughts.

God's endeavor is to equip his people to be strong. To do this, he has purposely shared his thoughts so we can know what action is wise or foolish. Thus, when consistently tempted in a given area, his children need to ingrain his advice in their minds. For example, if you are plagued with worry, go to Scripture and find God's thoughts on that subject. Commit to memory verses like Philippians 4:6, 7. At the very least, write out the passage on a 3" x 5" card and carry it with you at all times.

Then when you sense the temptation is at hand, quickly bring back the instructions of your Friend:

"Have no anxiety about anything, but in everything by prayer and supplication with thanksgiving let your requests be made known to God. And the peace of God, which passes all understanding, will keep your hearts and your minds in Christ Jesus."

The battle will be won in those early seconds, in that moment you decide to trust the counsel of your friend which you have just reviewed, or to follow the enticement of the enemy.

If your persistent problem is one of holding grudges, spend time in the Scriptures discovering God's thoughts on the topic. Choose a representative passage like Matthew 18: 21, 22, where Peter asks Christ, "Lord, how often shall my brother sin against me, and I forgive him? As many as seven times?"

Jesus responds, "I do not say to you seven times, but seventy times seven." Write it down. Better yet, start memorizing it. The next time the temptation to nurse a grudge appears, quickly clarify the difference between what the enemy is saying as opposed to what Christ had declared, and choose whose suggestion you will heed. Peter's advice, of course, is that in order to be alert during temptation one must trust a friend.

Let's review: *Satan's desire is to destroy; your opportunity is to overcome; and God's endeavor is to equip.*

God has seen to it that you need not just remain on the defensive. Your sword is this word from God. Learn to use it even as Christ did in the wilderness. Three swift thrusts, and the Scripture reports that "the devil left him" (Matt. 4:11). God has no desire that his people be victimized by the opposition. Frequent capitulation occurs because so few today discipline themselves in the use of spiritual weapons. "Trust the Lord," writes Peter; *God's endeavor is to equip.*

"Is that all you can offer by the way of help?" you ask. "Read the Bible and apply it?"

No, but for sure it's the starting point! And if you haven't done this much, I hesitate to give further instructions. What I am trying to do, when temptation is near, is to move you away from the question, "What will I do?" I want you to ask instead, "Whom will I trust?"

This is especially important to remember when you have the record that your Friend has once and for all brought the enemy to his knees. He is a lion tamer par excellence.

"But," you say, "what if the cat pounces on me from my blind side, and I fall before having a chance to think about whose advice I should follow?"

My reply is to advise you to concentrate on the major temptations you do see coming. As you experience victory in these situations, you will be better prepared to meet the sneak attacks. In the meantime, don't let the enemy discourage you regarding what is a relatively minor issue. Confess such sins, and then just put the event out of your mind.

5

GOD IS WATCHING

Has a current prevailing attitude affected your thinking? It goes something like this: Righteousness by its very nature is dull and uninteresting, but sin is synonymous with all that is delightful and exciting. The Christian life is available only in black and white, but what the enemy has to offer comes in living color and wraparound sound.

Fortunately in my day, I have seen many firsthand illustrations of the results of God's laws being flaunted and I have also observed those who have for years walked close to the Lord. All told, I feel that nowadays the truth is too often obscured. The average magazine short story or half-hour television vignette isn't long enough, or possibly honest enough, to reveal the heartbreak and guilt and dehumanization associated in real life with infidelity, selfishness, or bloodshed. When godliness is painted as lackluster or old-fashioned, it is because it's being presented by those who have never personally experienced the joy of an intimate friendship with God.

My desire, then, is to take the next three chapters to emphasize the following: *There is far greater benefit in overcoming temptation than in submitting to it.*

Let's examine the life of someone who faced a number of the same problems confronting people today. His name was Joseph, and his story is found in the first book of the Bible, Genesis. It begins in chapter 37 and concludes with chapter 50. In my Bible that is only seventeen pages; therefore, I don't think it is asking too much to request that you take time to read through this section as soon as possible. Your cooperation means I can illustrate from the story without taking time to retell it.

Right now I want to share three obvious temptations that Joseph faced; what he would have lost had he yielded to any of them; and finally, an obvious benefit that was his for choosing to overcome. In chapter 6 I'll follow the same pattern as we examine several aspects of the story that are not quite as apparent, and in chapter 7, I'd like to speculate a little. But let's start with the obvious.

When you think of Joseph (being sold into slavery as a seventeen-year-old by his brothers because of their jealousy) there is one obvious temptation he must have faced. One can hardly miss it: it's the desire for revenge.

He could have said: "Do you know what it is like to be a slave, to stand naked while someone examines you as though you were an animal, to say 'yes, sir, yes, sir' whenever your name is called, to forfeit any thought of the future? I guess you don't! But if I ever get my way, dear brothers, you will!" Such thoughts on our hero's part certainly would have been understandable.

The fact is, it wasn't only his brothers who did Joseph wrong. The wife of his slave-master attempted to seduce this handsome young Hebrew, and furious when he refused her, she had him jailed for years. Then a fellow prisoner for whom Joseph had done a favor conveniently forgot to repay the kindness upon his release.

What makes the narrative most interesting is the fact that Joseph is given the opportunity to revenge himself on all these people. At age thirty he is released from confinement and made the assistant to Pharaoh throughout all of Egypt. You'll see his importance as you read the narrative. In your imagination, watch as a chariot rolls into the government headquarters, dust billowing out behind it. It's young Joseph who reins his team to a halt. Now observe the license plate as the air clears— number two!

Obviously, he's in a great position to set matters right with his previous tormentors if he so desires. To revenge himself will provide certain benefits: a feeling of power, a sense of justice, the joy of getting even, pleasure in finally outsmarting an enemy. But whatever the advantages yielding to vengeance could afford, Joseph chose to believe there was far greater benefit in overcoming this temptation.

Another apparent allurement in the story is one hinted at already—sexual lust. Joseph was probably eighteen or nineteen when he was purchased by

Potiphar, an officer of Pharaoh. Scripture reports,

> And he made him overseer in his house and put him in charge of all that he had. . . . Now Joseph was handsome and goodlooking. And after a time his master's wife cast her eyes upon Joseph and said, "Lie with me." But he refused. . . . And although she spoke to Joseph day after day, he would not listen to her (Gen. 39:5-10).

Who knows the tremendous pressures represented in these verses. "Come Joseph, be over the whole house, . . . I mean, really be over the whole house!"

There are a couple of matters we need to notice. First, the woman was probably attractive. The Egyptians had a keen eye for beauty, and if she had been a slouch I doubt whether Potiphar would have become enraged when he was told what had allegedly happened. Second, Joseph was at an age when this specific temptation would have been extremely difficult. At the peak of his natural drives and curiosity, he was in a position where his ties with the past were severed. For all practical purposes, the influence of his upbringing could now be counted as nil. And who would know the difference? Third, had Joseph been savoring impure thoughts about this woman he probably would have fallen. Too often a person fails when confronted by the deed because in his thought-life defenses have been so weakened there is nothing left with which to resist.

Instead of submitting, however, Joseph's response was to flee and get out of the house. Probably most sophisticated men today would call him foolish. Look what he passed up: love, physical gratification, a sense of conquest, future secret times together, lifelong memories—this is the modern viewpoint in similar situations.

Joseph had another perspective. His words were, "My master has kept back nothing from me in this house, except yourself, because you are his wife; how then can I do this great wickedness, and sin against God?" In a little while you can judge for yourself as to whether or not he was wise in acting as he did.

One final area of conflict can hardly be missed by the casual reader. For a number of years, Joseph appeared to be a poor insurance risk. Some people would say he had a string of bad luck. No matter how hard he tried, he always seemed to end up the victim of some heinous plot against him. One event over which he had no control after another occurred and all seemed to thwart the fulfillment of what he held most dear.

I presume many readers can identify with Joseph. Believing strongly that a promise from God has come to you, you see exactly the opposite unfolding. This was Joseph's experience for thirteen years. And of course, the temptation in the darkness is to abandon what God has revealed to you in the light.

Without doubt most of us would enjoy being the favorite son of the father who gave him a multicolored uniform of prestige back in Canaan, but we would look with extreme dismay at the course of events that leave us languishing and forgotten in an Egyptian jail house. Circumstances don't necessarily make a person. More often, they reveal what the nature of the individual truly is. Joseph didn't spend his time grousing or pouting or trying to engender pity or saying, "I've had it, God. You can get someone else to practice faith; I'm finished praying to a deity who is hard of hearing!"

I suppose people with such an attitude learn to enjoy their rebellion. They get comfort by telling others how bad things have been for them. They cling tightly to stories of hardship and mistreatment. Joseph was not like this. He opted for another course.

What I'm stressing is: There is far greater benefit in overcoming temptation than in submitting to it. Whatever pluses are derived from getting even, or illicit sex, or despairing over adverse circumstances, see if they compare to the following. First, Joseph is made second to the Egyptian Pharaoh. He holds that position of favor until his death some eighty years later. He lives to see God's promises to him fulfilled when his family is reunited. And he, as was revealed by the Lord, holds the place of greatest respect.

But unless you're a Bible scholar, you might not realize that Joseph was to become the most detailed type of Christ in all of Scripture. Both stories, Christ's and Joseph's, follow the same pattern of the beloved of the Father being humbled and then exalted:

Loved. Like Christ, Joseph in obedience to his father sought his lost brethren, announced they were to bow to him, and he was met, as was Christ, by violence because the rule of love was misunderstood.

Humbled. Like Jesus, Joseph was hated by his own, without cause. A plot was hatched to do away with him. He was sold for so many pieces of silver. Both experienced great suffering and were counted as dead.

Exalted. Both Christ and Joseph take position at the right hand of the throne. Joseph, typifying what was to be Christ's experience, was given a Gentile bride and the government was laid upon his shoulders. He offered the world the bread of life, wept for his brothers in spite of their sin, and longed to draw them to himself. It's a beautiful picture.

Though Joseph wasn't aware this privilege was to be his, what a tragedy to have missed being the most perfect type of Jesus in all of Scripture.

Basically, this is the thrust of my remarks to you also. Whatever the pleasures your pet sin affords, my friend, you won't find it matches the joys of victory.

6

BENEFITS OF VICTORY

A mistake Christians often make is to naively refuse to admit there is a certain thrill to every sin. Those who yield to temptation generally don't grumble, "Oh, my! I suppose I'm going to have to do that bad thing again. How boring!" Not at all. Each sin affords a certain gratification. That is why people respond to its allure.

People outside the church often make a similar mistake, however. They do not realize that being godly also affords pleasure. Christians don't say, "I choose to do right even though it's dreadfully dull." I contend that there is far greater benefit to overcoming temptation than in submitting to it. That's the theme I began to develop in the last chapter. You also recall I requested that you read Genesis 37 through 50. this is the record of Joseph, the person whose life I'm using as an example.

Now you simply need to ask, "What temptation seems to be especially hard for me right now?" After you have that in mind, whether overindulgence, lack of control of your temper, selfishness, or immoral thoughts, I would like you to identify with Joseph and examine whether he was better off to submit to or resist the opportunities he had to sin.

We already have looked at temptations that were obvious in the scriptural account: seeking revenge, sexual immorality, and falling prey to despair because of a continuing string of adverse circumstances.

At this point, I'd like to mention three more temptations that are at the heart of the Joseph story, but maybe a little less apparent. The first would be becoming overwhelmed by a spiritual aloneness. Some of you might strongly identify with this difficulty, "I think I'm the only Christian in our entire school." "To bow my head and pray before eating at the factory is like taking on the scorn of the entire world." "My heart yearns for spiritual fellowship through the week, but there's no one around." Then you know a little of how Joseph felt when he was sold as a slave into Egypt at the young age of seventeen. There was no organization for young Hebrews in this foreign land, no religious broadcasts, not even a synagogue to attend. I doubt if things are that bad in most of our settings.

On the other hand, how impressive this wealthy country must have seemed to the new visitor. The famous preacher T. DeWitt Talmage writes,

The Egyptian capital was the focus of the world's wealth. In ships and barges there was brought to it: from India, frankincense, cinnamon, ivory and diamonds; from the north, marble and iron; from Syria, purple and silk; from Greece, some of the finest horses of the world and the most brilliant chariots; and from all the earth, that which could please the eye, charm the ear, and gratify the taste.

As you stand on the level beach of the sea on a summer day and look each way, there are miles of breakers, white with the ocean foam, dashing shoreward; so it seemed the sea of the world's power and wealth in the Egyptian capital for miles and miles flung itself up into white breakers of marble, temple, mausoleum, and obelisk.

After a while, does an unknown slave not say, "God, it's too much to expect of me. Here no one even knows your name. When the way of this magnificent society conflicts with your thoughts, I'm not sure I can always be loyal. There is a lot of pressure to conform, you know. The advantages to adapting are a sense of belonging, friendships galore, less resistance to me as a person—and you must admit, that in my present situation those are large rewards."

You'll find when you read the story that Joseph refused to compromise. His first words before Pharaoh are typical of his thinking. When brought from years of prison life into the presence of probably the most powerful man in the world of that day, and asked if he could interpret dreams, Joseph responded, "It's not in me. God will give Pharaoh a favorable answer."

The temptation to adjust to one's surroundings because of spiritual aloneness would not defeat Joseph!

Quite closely related is another common flaw, the lack of spiritual endurance. Some people hold out admirably for a while, but repeated attacks seem to wear them down. The temptation, then, is to quit because of weariness or exhaustion. "How long can you take it, Joseph, without turning on a God who remains so strangely silent even through the shock of your brothers' hatred, the endless miles of hot desert sands you walked as a slave, when they stripped you in the slave market? You were just getting situated as the head steward in Potiphar's house and now you're thrown in jail because of righteously refusing the sexual advances of his wife. What kind of justice is that? Pharaoh's butler, a fellow prisoner, is released, promising to put in a good word for you, but he forgets. And the years grind on and on and on. Now you are thirty years old. How long is one expected to keep the faith in the face of such storms?"

Have you ever felt like just giving up? That following Christ is too painful? Question: Who eventually put the dream about the fat and the lean cows in the mind of the sleeping Egyptian monarch that resulted in Joseph's exaltation? That's right. God did! Have you ever wondered why He didn't do it sooner? He certainly could have. The only reason I can determine for not doing so is that Joseph apparently wasn't ready for the job ahead.

James writes in the New Testament, "Count it all joy, my brethren, when you meet various trials, for you know that the testing of your faith produces steadfastness. And let steadfastness have its full effect, that you may be perfect and complete, lacking in nothing" (James 1:2-4).

The patient believer becomes a great rock which storms beat against but are helpless to break. What advantages would Joseph have gained in yielding to the temptation of throwing in the towel? Less pressure to be someone special? The strange pleasures of self-pity? Not having to take life quite so seriously? Further than that I find it hard to speculate.

One final pitfall needs examining before we look at a unique joy that was reserved for this man in his overcoming. As you know, when Joseph unfolded the riddle of Pharaoh's dream that there would be seven years of plenty followed by seven years of famine, he was raised to the position of second to the throne. It's safe to assume that for someone who's been deprived for a good part of his life, another temptation would be faced—pride. "Well, folks, give a gander at where your old daddy is now all of a sudden!"

What is pride? It's an unwholesome focusing on self, a haughtiness or arrogance, an obsession with "who I am and what I've accomplished, and what is mine and the concerns I have." Are there benefits to yielding to this enticement? Yes, many people find subtle strutting to be great fun: if you've got it, flaunt it! It feels good to be on top, especially since everyone else recognizes that's where you're sitting.

But if Joseph stumbled here, it certainly isn't indicated in Scripture. Rather, his words show a continued awareness that *the Lord* is the one responsible for what he had become. "God . . . made me a father to Pharaoh, and lord of all his house and ruler over all the land of Egypt" (Gen. 45:8).

Possibly Joseph chose to shun the profits afforded by pride because he knew, as I've been saying, that *there is far greater benefit in overcoming temptation than in submitting to it.* I can't say for sure, but I can unfold from Scripture another of the pluses that accrued to his account for having been faithful through so many trials.

A most electrifying paragraph is found at the end of Genesis, chapter 41. It reads, "And the seven years of famine began to come, as Joseph had said. . . . Moreover, *all the earth* came to Egypt to Joseph to buy grain, because the famine was severe over all the earth" (vv. 54, 57).

"What's so exciting about that?" you ask.

Well, many years back God had given young Joseph a promise in a dream. One day all his family would bow before him, and he was to have a unique position above his brothers and even his father. Now the time had finally come for the Almighty to fulfill his promise. And in order to do so, God was willing to involve the entire population of the known world in famine.

Why this terrible hunger and its awful scope? So that God could vindicate His word to faithful Joseph. And before long, ten brothers will be sent from Canaan by their aged father to Egypt for food, because they too have felt the pinch of hunger. The very first thing they will do upon seeing this one they betrayed will be to bow before him with their faces to the ground.

Remember the lad's dream? "Behold, we were binding sheaves in the field, and lo, my sheaf arose and stood upright; and behold, your sheaves gathered around it, and bowed down to my sheaf." At that time his brothers mocked him: "Are you indeed to reign over us?"

Later even old Jacob, Israel himself, will travel the caravan route and live under his son's authority just as predicted.

How would you like to see God's hand operating like that in the affairs of men and nations just to show himself true on *your* behalf? How would you like to experience other great thrills of overcoming temptations, in comparison to the cheap benefits known by those who too quickly give in?

Because I believe when it's understood that greater joy characterizes those who follow close after God, tongues will be checked from their normal vindictiveness, worry will be rechanneled into prayer, pride will be put down when it rears its head, and even the matter that has been hassling you will be less a problem than before. Instead of defeat and guilt, you'll experience the taste of victory and joy. May it be so!

7

BATTLING BENEATH THE SURFACE

I was raised near Hannibal, Missouri, and heard a lot about Mark Twain, one of America's favorite authors. You undoubtedly recall the famous episode told in his *Adventures of Tom Sawyer* in which the hero tricks his friends into whitewashing the fence for him, getting them to think the work he had to do was great fun. We laugh when we read this section, because we know Tom had to be quite a con artist to pull off such a prank—turning a job he hated into a privilege for which his friends would beg.

I have been attempting to expose a similar reversal of realities. Somehow people have adopted the mistaken idea that sin is always exciting and glamorous, while godliness is dull and uninteresting. While it may be right to do good, it certainly is an unfortunate draw if that is what you've chosen as your lot. My contention, however, is that *there is far greater benefit in overcoming temptation than in submitting to it.* This advantage not only relates to the life to come but to the present as well.

This is not to say that sin has no appeal. If they did not receive gratification of one kind or another, people would stop lying or cheating or lusting or stealing or being selfish. But too few are aware that overcoming such flaws brings pleasure also, including self-respect, a spirit of confidence, even immediate happiness and joy, better interpersonal relationships and a strong sense of God's presence. Therefore, my words have been intended to line up your thinking with what is indeed the truth.

My approach has been not to argue the case intellectually, but rather to simply look at the account of one whose opportunities for wrong were multiple. Not that this isn't the case with all of us, but the path of Joseph seemed to put him in extreme positions of pain and privilege, despair but also great dignity. He was probably tempted beyond what most of us have known.

We have looked at the obvious testings of Joseph's life in Genesis 37 through 50 (seeking revenge, indulging in sexual lust, or sinking in despair under the mounting weight of adverse circumstances). The obvious pluses that were his because he didn't submit to these vices were: being awarded the position of honor just below Pharaoh for eighty years, the prophesied role of respect in his family becoming his, and above all the breathtaking privilege of being the most perfect type of Christ in all of Scripture.

Then we again examined Joseph's life and a little beneath the surface saw him battling pride, aloneness, and the temptation of quitting too soon. Coming out victorious, however, he experienced the thrill of having God involve the total world of that day in a program of famine just so his earlier word to Joseph could be vindicated. Years before, the Lord had said in a dream that all in Joseph's family were to bow before him. Now the Lord was unfolding events on a world scale so that in Canaan the family of Jacob would get hungry enough to travel to Egypt where plenty of grain had been stored. Arriving on Joseph's turf, one of the first things his brothers would do would be to bow on their faces before him exactly as God had promised. Before long, even the father, Jacob, would travel to Egypt to live under the governing skills of his son he thought was dead. I don't know if the details of God moving in the events of the world to prove Himself faithful to one person captured you as I shared it, but they said to my heart: Certainly the benefits of overcoming temptation were greater than anything Joseph could have known had he yielded to the allurements. And I'm going to believe the same is true for me!

Such review is helpful because it gives a stamp of validity to what I'll share now. You see, I'd like to speculate just a bit as we visit with Joseph one final time. Let's reverse the procedure for a change and talk first of the benefit of faithfulness before looking at the trials.

As the New Testament begins, God is again in need of a man to whom he can speak in dreams as he did to the one we're studying. The Lord was looking for someone who when hurt deeply by the person he loved the most (this time his wife-to-be) would not strike back in revenge. For this man was also called just. He would be a person whose normal course of life was disrupted by circumstances beyond his control, a man who could experience the spiritual aloneness of Egypt and still maintain his faith, a gentleman who would refrain from premature sexual involvement, who was humble and not proud. He, though vitally important, must always remain second to another who was the real ruler. Here was to be the closest male to God's Son, the Lord Jesus Christ.

This man was to fill the teaching role by word and action as stepfather to Jesus, God's only begotten son. Because the qualifications so closely parallel the one at whom we've been looking, I don't believe it was without significance that he was called by his parents at birth by the same name, Joseph. It seems to me that here is one final tribute of blessing ordained by God for this character we've been studying. Sure it's speculation, but it's almost as though God said, "Because I want a man like you to play for me the role of my Son's earthly father, not only will I pick one with the good qualities you exhibited, I'll also see to it that he bears your name— Joseph!"

If it's all the same to you, I'd like also to speculate a little regarding some possible temptations that our Old Testament Joseph had to overcome. And if you face similar ones, just remind yourself that at least for this man there was far greater benefit in subduing than submitting.

The first temptation might have been to become so busy in his new responsibilities that he failed to keep his spiritual priorities. Consider this verse, "Joseph stored up grain in great abundance, like the sand of the sea, until he ceased to measure it, for it couldn't be measured" (Gen. 41:49). Because of the press such responsibility must have brought on, I'm sure the enemy placed thoughts in his mind such as: The fact that the Lord wants you to play some ill-defined role in the life of His people really isn't that important in comparison to what you're doing right now. So, why not let spiritual disciplines take a back seat for a while, at least until the pressure is off!

I bring up the point because I've talked to people with far less responsibility than Joseph had who have fallen prey to the peril of being so involved in what they're doing that they no longer seem to have time to pursue their relationship with the Lord. Over a period of weeks, months, and years, a noticeable change marks their lives.

Could you be one who needs to ask yourself, "What really are my priorities?" Do you need to plan how you can rearrange your schedule around the Lord instead of constantly fitting him in when you have a chance?

"These hours are reserved for church."

"This time on this night I'll set aside for Scripture."

"Here's when I'll talk with the Lord."

Once the urgency of these items is established and honored, what follows is easy. It's called beating the dilemma of daily demands. After all, what valuable compensations come from being a workaholic anyway?

Because Joseph's term in office was so long, I presume after a while there was also a temptation to live in the past. "I've played my role. Examine the record, and you'll see my contribution." A continual mulling over of an earlier string of spiritual successes can be comforting.

I know people like this. They retire spiritually at the same time they do vocationally. "From now on, I'm doing what *I* want and nobody is going to make demands on me anymore." Though they don't specifically say it, that statement includes God also.

Not so with Joseph. He is included among the heroes of faith in Hebrews 11, and it states that he mentioned the Exodus and gave directions concerning his burial. Read his words in Genesis 50, "I am about to die; but God will visit you, and bring you up out of this land to the land which he swore to Abraham, to Isaac, and to Jacob. Then Joseph took an oath of the sons of Israel, saying, 'God will visit you and you shall carry up my bones from here'" (vv. 24, 25). In identifying at all times with what the Lord was doing, even after his spirit departed, Joseph's body was to be a reminder of God's continuing work among his people. There was no living in the past for this man.

One final thought. There might have been a temptation for Joseph to attempt to spare his children the pain he had experienced following Jehovah. Certainly there is peace of mind in knowing your offspring are comfortable and cared for. Not that they would serve other gods, but that their lives would be protected, if possible, from the struggle and hurt associated with following hard after God.

But before he dies, Grandfather Jacob requests that Joseph's two sons, Ephraim and Manasseh, be his, even as Reuben and Simeon are. Hence they are to become an integral part of the continuing story of God's people in the days ahead.

"Maybe," Joseph thought (wondering with foresight if

some day his sons' children might not thus be among those to suffer making bricks in the clay pits under afflicting taskmasters) "Dad Jacob, I'm not certain this is what I want. I'd like, if possible, to spare them the trials that I've gone through. Why not let them stay here in Egypt?"

But now, for his children and grandchildren, he was willing to say no to the titles, friends, possessions, security, the way of life of Egypt and identify fully with God's plans for the Hebrews in Canaan.

Well, it's a beautiful man we've been studying, but just as wonderful is the truth he modeled that can be ours today as well. There is far greater benefit to overcoming temptation than in submitting to it.

8

A REMARKABLE CONSIDERATION

Many people are confident they have experienced forgiveness through Christ but seem unable to overcome sin in their lives. You too may feel assured that through Christ's death and resurrection you have been forgiven the wrongs you have done, but still you cannot cope with temptation on a day-to-day basis. You are grateful for the peace you have with God but you long for *power* when it comes to rubbing shoulders with evil. I suggest that the basic problem could be in the way you *think*, because you might not be aware that Christ's work made victory possible for his followers just as it made forgiveness available to them.

In his epistle to the Romans, the Apostle Paul addressed this point. He talks, in the first part of his letter, about the work of Christ in relationship to our position of guilt before the Lord. Having settled the fact that our pardon comes through faith in Christ's work on Calvary, and not by means of self-effort or good deeds, the apostle then examines the question of our continuing life in the flesh.

Should we expect to keep on doing evil following our conversion? "By no means!" Paul answers. He continues:

> How can we who died to sin still live in it? Do you not *know* that all of us who have been baptized into Christ Jesus were baptized into his death? We were buried therefore with him in baptism into death, so that as Christ was raised from the dead by the glory of the Father, we too might walk in newness of life.
>
> We *know* that our old self was crucified with him so that the sinful body might be destroyed, and we might no longer be enslaved to sin. For he who has died is freed from sin. . . . For we *know* that Christ being raised from the dead will never die again; death no longer has dominion over him. The death he died he died to sin, once for all, but the life he lives he lives to God. So you also must consider yourselves dead to sin and alive to God in Christ Jesus (Rom. 6:2, 9-11).

The fact he's stressing is that Christians who understand that Christ made forgiveness of sin possible must also know that he broke the power of sin over their lives as well. Possibly, an illustration would help at this point.

Watchman Nee in his classic, *The Normal Christian Life,* puts it this way:

> Suppose, for the sake of illustration, that the government of your country should wish to deal drastically with the

question of strong drink and should decide the whole country was to go "dry." How could the decision be carried into effect? If we were to search every shop and house throughout the land and smash all the bottles of wine or beer or brandy we came across, would that meet the case? Surely not. We might thereby rid the land of every drop of alcoholic liquor it contains, but behind those bottles of strong drink are the factories that produced them, and if we only deal with the bottles and leave the factories untouched, production will still continue and there is no permanent solution of the problem. No, the drink-producing factories, the breweries and distilleries throughout the land must be closed down if the drink question is ever to be effectively and permanently settled.

Well, the blood of the Lord Jesus dealt with the question of the products, namely our sins. So the question of what we have done is settled; but would God have stopped there? What about the question of what we are? Our sins have been produced by us. They have been dealt with, but how are we going to be dealt with? Do you believe the Lord would cleanse away all our sins and leave us to get rid of the sin-producing factory?

To ask this question is but to answer it. Of course He has not done half the work and left the other half undone. No, He has done away with the goods and also made a clean sweep of the factory that produced the goods.

The finished work of Christ really has gone to the root of our problem and dealt with it. There are no half measures with God. He has made full provision for sin's rule to be utterly broken.

"Knowing this," says Paul, "that our old man was crucified with him . . . we should no longer be in bondage to sin." *Knowing* this! Yes, but do you know it? Or are you ignorant? (Christian Literature Crusade, 1957, p. 41).

Nee illustrates what Paul set forth in Romans, namely, that at Calvary Christ was not only the perfect sacrifice whose blood atoned for our sin, he was also the great conqueror who in the very lair of the enemy soundly defeated him. Because of Christ's work, Satan is now a beaten foe. Christ is the victor and sin no longer rightfully has power over those who identify with him.

What effect does this have on your life? Throughout Scripture faith is always built on truth—God's truth. For example, you can't sense forgiveness from God if you don't *know* the fact that Christ's death made this possible. However, once the truth has penetrated your mind you can in faith respond to it and forgiveness becomes yours. The proportion of your sin doesn't matter once you see that Christ's death means cleansing is personally available for you. It is a matter of appropriating his great gift to yourself by faith. But *knowing the fact* makes it possible to act upon it!

I believe that too few Christians are aware that Christ also literally broke the power of sin over us when he died on our behalf. In Nee's terms, "He crushed the very source of evil." And Watchman Nee is only reiterating Paul's thought from Romans. But if this is not realized, if it is not understood or known, faith has no way of being born, nor can this truth become operative in the heart.

Maybe you are one who was conditioned to failure by words from a friend. "Well, Jesus can forgive your sin, but don't expect your life to change drastically just because his spirit lives in you. Mine certainly didn't."

If some well-meaning, but ignorant, person talks to you like this, the following can be extremely helpful:

Knowing Christ defeated the power of sin frees his followers to consider themselves dead to it as well. If that sounds too extreme, here is Romans 6:11 again: "So you also must consider yourselves dead to sin and alive to God in Christ Jesus."

Let's see if I can illustrate by relating to your experience. You became a Christian on the basis of faith in the person and work of Christ. But, say, you didn't realize at the time that Jesus also broke the power of sin over your life. In the flush of release from your burden you probably then began a pattern that, though admirable, was basically self-effort. When tempted, you said, "I shouldn't do that; it wouldn't be fair to Christ after he's done so much for me." But the focus of your struggle while facing temptation was on yourself. "Will *I* be strong enough?" "*I* need help." "What will *I* do?"

I hope that, through discipline, you were often the winner. But as time went on, the frequency of temptation or the power of several especially difficult problems consistently overcame you. So now it appears that certain sins will cling to you for life. There seems to be no hope for anything better.

I want to share with you the good news that Christ has also made victory possible for you, including defeat over the very sins that seem to shackle you. Lying, lack of self-control, profanity, selfishness. According to Scripture, all of these have been stripped of their power by Christ in his work at Calvary. As you read the Word and allow this fact to become firmly planted in your mind, your walk to freedom has begun. For once you *know* that Christ has broken the power of sin over your life, you can begin to respond in faith to that truth.

By way of practical application, the next time you are tempted don't focus on yourself but quickly turn your mind to this reality—that in his marvelous work at Calvary Christ defeated the power of this precise sin which troubles you.

Maybe self-pity has been rolling in on you today. Remember that Christ stripped this indulgence of feeling sorry for yourself of any power over you when he died and rose again. He made it possible that no Christian would have to fall victim to such a force again.

Are you always stretching the truth to make yourself look better? You've been doing it for years and it's taken a great toll. When you're next tempted, realize you don't have to submit to this problem, because Jesus destroyed its power to enslave you when he died and rose again.

Can one ever overcome lustful thoughts? In yourself you probably can't. Deliberately set your mind on Christ during this temptation, however, because he defeated lust's coils when he submitted to the test of the cross and the tomb. A part of that great battle was the question of whether impure thoughts were going to be able to hold people like yourself forever captive. I know as a fact that Christ won that decisive conflict, and you can now claim identity with his victory and walk away from this temptation.

Do you see the pattern? Instead of being obsessed with the problem and your lack of strength to overcome it, at the initial sign of the tempter center your mind on Christ and his complete victory and on the truth that through identification with him you too can overcome.

"Ah," you say, "that's just a little mental trick and I

know it's not going to work."

Well, it's a bit presumptuous for you to say it won't work if you have never tried it! Granted, I am only suggesting that you think differently about temptation. However, the thought process is based on the single most important truth we have in this world—namely, that God sent his Son to enable us to be restored to him *and to walk a totally new way!* Once the magnitude of that statement captures your mind, you will never again unwittingly excuse sin or see temptation as overpowering.

"Do you then think human beings can be perfect?" you ask.

No, I have experienced enough of the enemy's cleverness and my own slowness to learn that I don't entertain such a thought for a moment. But I do believe that a Christian should have a basic mindset of victory as opposed to one of defeat. An emphasis on self-effort doesn't foster sustained optimism. But by experience I can testify that knowing Christ defeated the power of sin frees his followers to consider themselves *dead* to it as well.

9

LITTLE THINGS MEAN A LOT

"Daddy, if you could have any wish you knew would come true, what would you ask for?" Having gone through this routine with four children, I now know that I'm supposed to pretend to think about it awhile, and then, obviously not wise enough to make such a momentous decision quickly, turn the question back to the child.

"That's very hard, Jeremy. What would you want?"

Hardly able to wait a moment longer, all smiles, bouncing from one foot to the other, he then reports what children have been saying down through the years, each sure nobody ever thought of such a clever answer. "I'd ask for a bunch more wishes!"

Maybe when I was younger I would have asked for that too. But as a man, more and more I realize that I actually need only one wish to cover my desires. Apart from the fact that my request might sound a little sanctimonious, I'm quite open to sharing with you what it is. In fact, what greater ambition could any created being have than to experience, like an Abraham, an intimate, sustained friendship with one's creator? That's what I'd pick!

A. W. Tozer expressed similar feelings in his book, *The Pursuit of God.*

> The moment the Spirit has quickened us to life in regeneration our whole being senses its kinship to God and leaps up in joyous recognition. This is the heavenly birth without which we cannot see the kingdom of God. It is, however, not an end, but an inception, for now begins the glorious pursuit, the heart's happy exploration of the infinite riches of the Godhead. This is where we begin, I say, but where we stop no man has yet discovered, for there is in the awful and mysterious depths of the triune God neither limit nor end.
>
> > Shoreless Ocean, who can sound Thee?
> > Thine own eternity is round Thee;
> > Majesty Divine!
>
> To have God and still to pursue Him, is the soul's paradox of love; scorned indeed by the too-easily satisfied religionist, but justified in happy experience by the children of the burning heart. St. Bernard stated this holy paradox in a musical quatrain that will be instantly understood by every worshiping soul:
>
> > We taste Thee, O Thou Living Bread,
> > And long to feast upon Thee still;
> > We drink of Thee, the Fountainhead
> > And thirst our souls from Thee to fill.

My single wish, then, is to know the Lord more intimately, to sense his presence in my life in ways beyond the beauty of what has been experienced to date, to trust him more, to enjoy a growing closeness with God.

Do you ever have similar feelings? If so, read carefully, because I've come far enough in this relationship to have discovered an important truth. The better acquainted I am with God, the more I'm aware of his insistence on holiness. This seems to be a matter about which he's not open to the slightest negotiating.

Oh, you could bring the subject up and say, "I think you're too stubborn on this issue, God. Now I've made some pretty big concessions to you. I would think that on this matter of sin you could compromise a little anyway." I'll guarantee he won't budge! The fact is, the privilege of intimacy with God carries with it an awareness that he places great significance on this truth.

I'm reminded of the words of the New Testament personality who was closest to Christ. His name was John, the apostle, and he wrote: "God is light and in him is no darkness at all. If we say we have fellowship with him while we walk in darkness, we lie and do not live according to the truth. . . . In him there is no sin, and no one who abides in him sins."

You recall Isaiah writing in the Old Testament: "In the year that King Uzziah died I saw the Lord sitting upon a throne, high and lifted up; and his train filled the temple. Above him stood the seraphim; . . . and one called to another" (do you remember what it was?) "Sovereign, sovereign is the Lord!" Right? No. "Omnipotent. Omnipotent." No. "All wise." That's still not it. They called:

"Holy, holy, holy is the Lord of hosts; the whole earth

is full of his glory." And the foundations of the threshold shook at the voice of him who called, and the house was filled with smoke. And I said: "Woe is me! For I am lost: for I am a man of unclean lips, and I dwell in the midst of a people of unclean lips; for my eyes have seen the King, the Lord of hosts!" (Isa. 6:3-5).

I have a suspicion, no, a conviction, that to draw near to God in any age is to come away with this same impression: *He is holy!*

This doesn't mean we can't know him as a friend. It only means he can never be thought of in that way exclusively. In *The Tales of Narnia,* by C.S. Lewis (Macmillan, 1970), the Christ figure is Aslan, the lion. He can be gentle and play and romp. "But be careful," warns the writer, "he's not a tame lion, you know!" With these words Lewis helps his readers understand there is another side to this personality that is awesome, to be respected, and even feared. The truth he thus captured figuratively is consistent with the picture of God in the sacred Scriptures. Yes, he's a friend who sticks closer than a brother, but he's also an all-consuming fire.

Some of the greatest saints, unfortunately, had to learn this lesson the hard way. Who worshiped the Lord as Israel's David did, a man after God's own heart? Yet he also found this privilege of intimacy was not to be taken for granted.

Who knew fellowship with God as Adam did? Closeness didn't insulate him from his Creator's judgement of his disobedience.

Who's been part of a church that could possibly compare to the one described in Acts 5? Yet, the nearness to God of members of that body was not a safety guarantee for Annanias and Sapphira when they lied, but their very destruction.

Walking with God doesn't allow for laxity regarding sin, even though such an unconscious attitude seems to characterize a good many of Christ's present disciples. It is as though that which damns people for eternity suddenly becomes palatable to God once one is born anew.

"How can it be such a big issue in our marriage?" your defensive spouse asks. "It's just a little thing between us, flirting now and then, that's all, you know. The great majority of my love is given to you. Isn't that enough?" But you're not satisfied with such reasoning, are you? Neither is God when those who say they seek to share his intimacy still make silly overtures toward His enemy. Believe me, little sins should loom bigger in your mind, not smaller, if you're really drawing close to him.

In that context, I'm reminded of Psalm 99. It begins with the majesty of God.

The Lord reigns: Let the peoples tremble! He sits enthroned upon the cherubim; let the earth quake! The Lord is great in Zion; he is exalted over all the peoples. Let them praise thy great and terrible name! Holy is he! Mighty king, lover of justice, thou hast established equity; thou hast executed justice and righteousness in Jacob. Extol the Lord our God; worship at his footstool! Holy is he!" (vv. 1-5).

Then it mentions specific men afforded the delight of knowing God well—three who were treated with his friendship: "Moses and Aaron were among his priests,

Samuel also was among those who called on his name. They cried to the Lord, and he answered them. He spoke to them in the pillar of cloud; they kept his testimonies, and the statutes that he gave them. O Lord our God, thou didst answer them; thou wast a forgiving God to them" (vv. 6-8).

What a privilege to have held such unique positions. But notice the end of verse 8: "An avenger of their wrongdoings"!

No, intimacy didn't carry with it immunity from divine discipline. Just the opposite was true. Why? Here's verse 9 in conclusion: "Extol the Lord our God, and worship at his holy mountain; for the Lord our God is holy!" That's the key. In a sentence, what I'm saying is; *To enjoy a closeness with God is to know his demand for holiness.*